Miss Pam's HERE!

OLYMPIC TORCH TRIUMPH

Written by Dan Freschi

Illustrations by Angela Ayala

Miss Pam's Here!
Miss Pam & Rosey - Olympic Torch Triumph

Written by Dan Freschi
Illustrated by Angela Ayala
Contributing Editor: Marla McKenna
Layout by Michael Nicloy

Paperback ISBN-13: 978-1-957351-80-3

Published by Nico 11 Publishing & Design
Mukwonago, Wisconsin
www.nico11publishing.com

Be well read.

Quantity orders may be placed with the publisher via email:
mike@nico11publishing.com

Printed in The United States of America

for more:
www.misspamshere.com

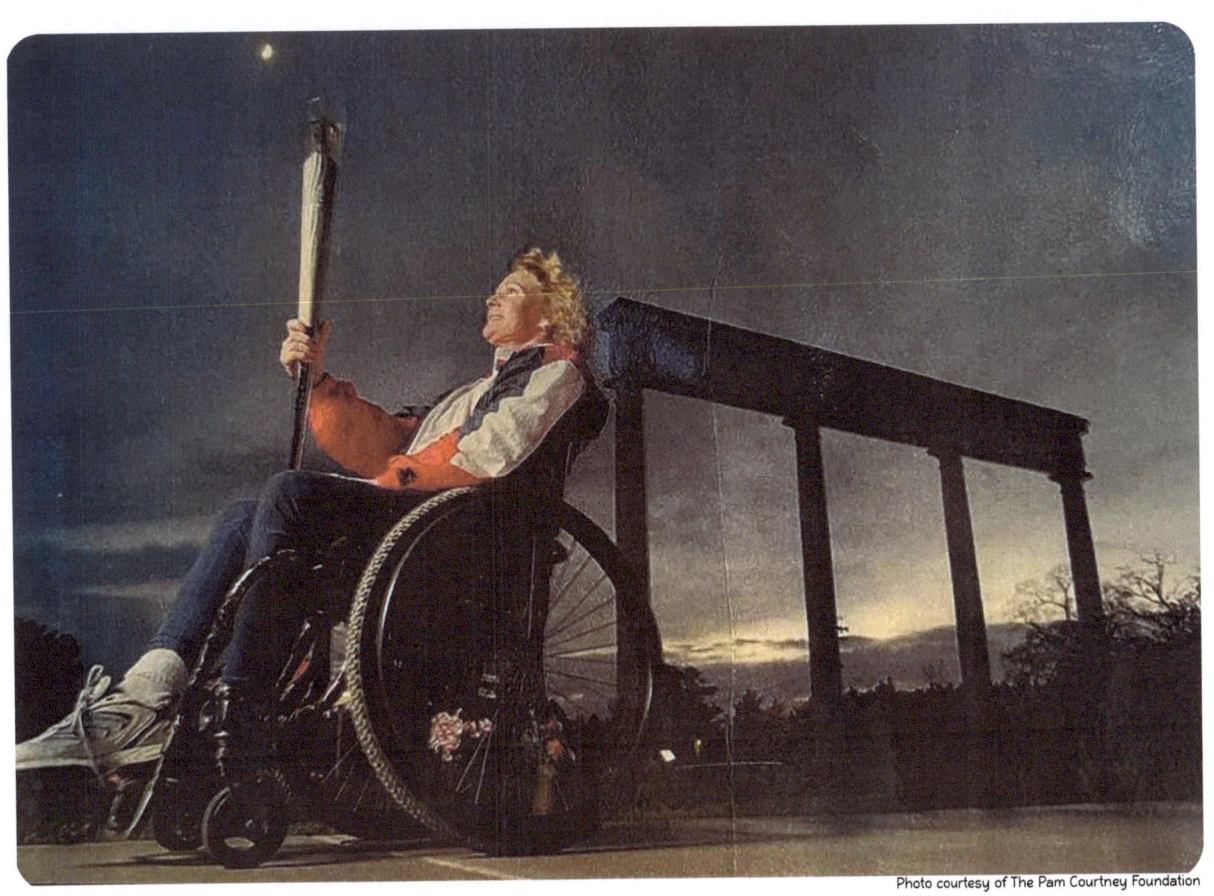

Pamela S. Courtney
September 7, 1959 - August 25, 2023

To the generations of children and families at
Hubert H. Bancroft Elementary, whose lives
were brightened by Miss Pam's joy, lifted by
her courage, and forever changed by her love.

In the heartwarming town of College Greens, there was a little, brick school named Bancroft Elementary. It was filled with so many wonderful and bright students. They learned how to read and write, multiply and divide, and how to count the stars in the night sky. (That's hard!) They also learned how to count the rings of a tree. (Much easier!)

They loved their teachers and learning, but sitting at their desks all day made them wiggly. They'd playfully tap their pencils and watch the minute hand slowly tick around the clock.

Finally!

PE!

It was time for
the best part of
the day – PE with
Miss Pam!

The students quickly lined up at their classroom door, and their teacher walked them to the gymnasium.

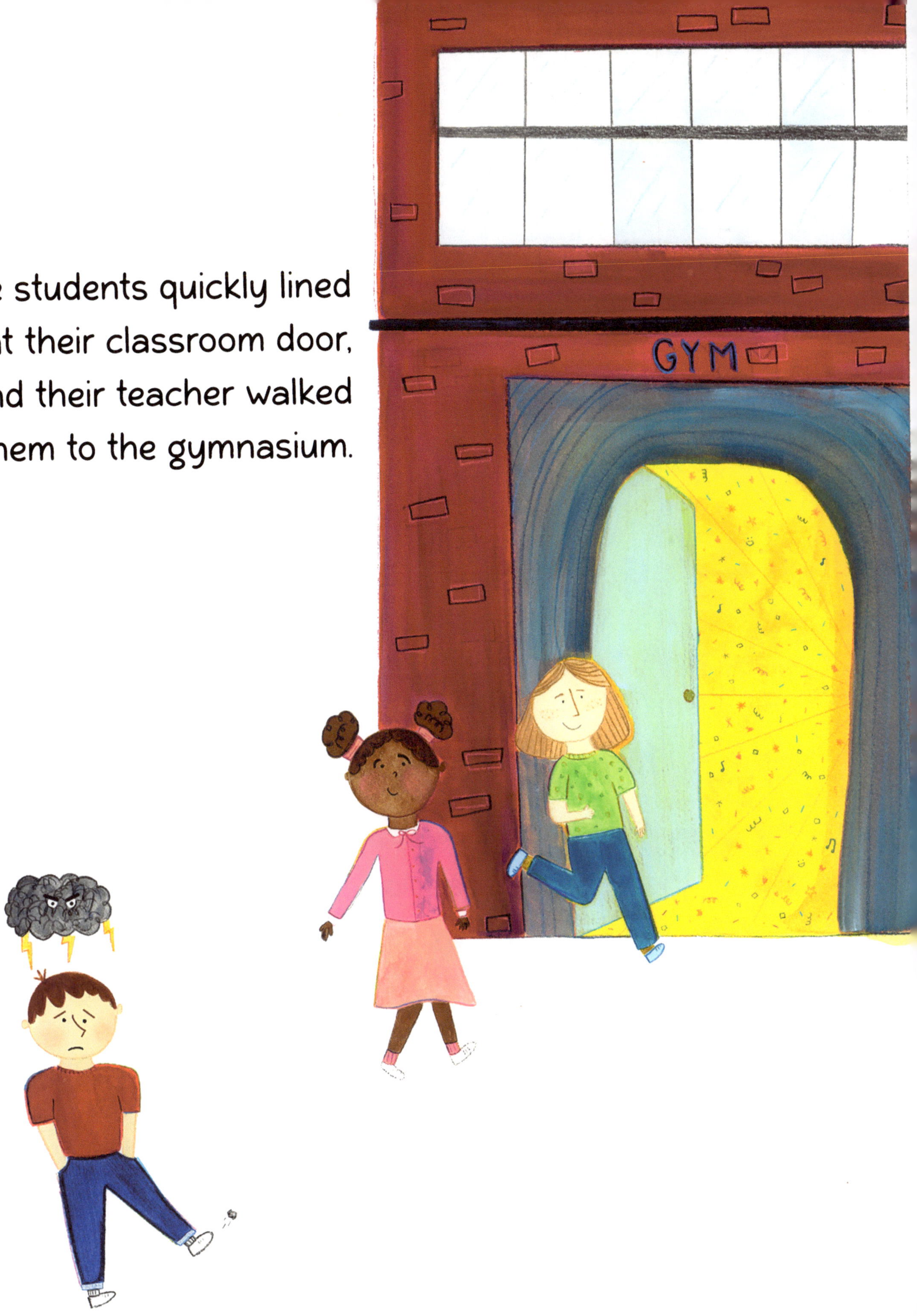

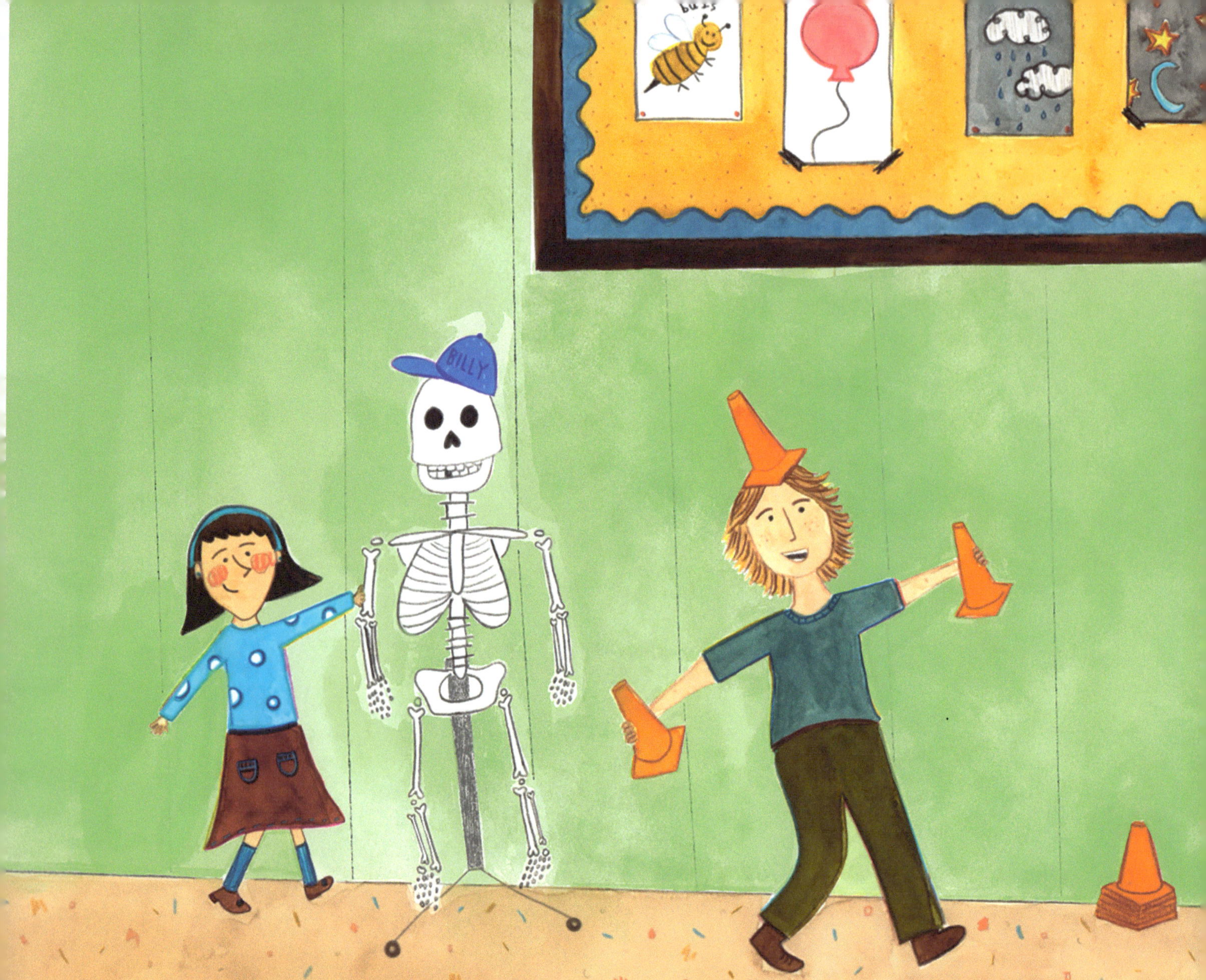

Once there, they began to find their spots on the colored carpet squares. Suddenly, Miss Pam rolled in singing "Helloooo," in her friendly, raspy voice.

the students
shouted with
excitement and cheers.

LUNCH MENU
Spaghetti!

WOOF!

"Hi, Miss Pam!"

"Hi, Rosey!"

Miss Pam taught all her classes from her wheelchair alongside her loyal pup and sidekick, Rosey.
A few 6th grade helpers followed closely behind holding orange rubber cones, a milk crate full of bright yellow and red fabric, and a large white board.

Once the giggling calmed down, Miss Pam continued to speak, "We're going to start playing Capture the Flag this week, but I have some things to go over with you first," as she straightened out the papers on her clipboard.

"First, we'll listen to some of your favorite music and do our warm-up exercises. Then, we'll go over the easy rules of Capture the Flag, pick teams by counting off by two, and then play for the rest of class.

"Sound good?"

"No, Miss Pam," Joseph mumbled, sadly.

"No?" Miss Pam asked, curiously.

"I don't want to," Joseph said in an unsure voice from the back of the gym. "I'm not very good at any of those things."

"Hmmmm ... " thought Miss Pam.

"Hmmmm ... " thought Rosey.

"Well, is that so? Then today, I want to share a special story with you," she said as her eyes gleamed with warmth and determination. "It's about never giving up, no matter what challenges life throws your way."

The students settled into their carpet squares, criss-cross applesauce, eagerly waiting to hear Miss Pam's story. Her stories were always soooo good. Rosey sat beside Miss Pam, tilting her head as she raised her ears to listen.

"Many years ago," Miss Pam started, "I was a Junior Olympic athlete. I loved running, biking, and competing. I had big dreams of competing in the Olympics."

The students were in awe - all eyes focused on Miss Pam. They knew Miss Pam loved sports, but they didn't know she had wanted to be in the Olympics!

"But one day, everything changed," Miss Pam went on to explain. "I was in a car accident and lost the use of my legs."

"After my accident," Miss Pam continued, "I felt discouraged. I felt like all the great things I wanted to accomplish in my life were no longer possible. But then, I realized I could still do great things, just in a different way. I started looking at my new challenges positively instead of negatively. And with the support of my loved ones and a lot of hard work, I am able to have a very full and fun life!"

The students nodded. Miss Pam's life did seem fun. She had shown them photos from her exciting summer trips, games, and concerts she'd attended.

Miss Pam was always laughing and smiling, and everyone around her seemed to be having fun, too!

"In fact, one of the best
moments of my life,"
Miss Pam continued
with a smile, "was when
I got to be in the Olympics!"

"Wait, I thought you said you couldn't
be in the Olympics!?" asked Sammy.

"I got to be in the Olympics in a different kind of way!"
Miss Pam laughed and encouraged.

"Years ago, my students secretly wrote letters to a group of important people asking that I be chosen to carry the Olympic torch through the streets of our special town.

"It was an incredible honor, and I couldn't believe I got to be part of the Olympics after all!"

It was a symbol of hope and perseverance.

The students were captivated by Miss Pam's story. They could picture her, strong and determined, carrying the Olympic torch with pride.

"But how did you carry the torch and use your wheelchair?" asked Michael, a bit curious and confused.

"My dad made me a special holder, so I could carry the torch and use my wheelchair," Miss Pam said.

"Were you nervous?" asked Alex, one of the 6th graders. "Yes, but I felt a powerful sense of accomplishment. It reminded me that even when we face obstacles, we can overcome them and achieve wonderful and great things. It's all about believing in ourselves and never giving up."

"Was Rosey there?" asked Hannah.

"Of course!" replied Miss Pam.

Christian raised his hand and asked, "Miss Pam, how did you keep going when things got tough?"

Miss Pam smiled warmly and said, "It wasn't easy, Christian. But I learned to focus on what I could do rather than what I couldn't. I set new goals for myself and worked hard to achieve them. Plus, I had wonderful support from my students, friends, family, and a community who believed in me, just like I believe in all of you."

"*And me!*" thought Rosey.
She barked at Miss Pam.

"Yes, Rosey, and you too."

Mary, another student, spoke up. "Wow! Miss Pam, you're such an inspiration!"

Martha agreed and said, "You're amazing!"

Miss Pam's eyes sparkled with gratitude.
"Thank you, Mary. Remember, each of you has the
power to overcome challenges and achieve your
dreams. Believe in yourselves and support each other,
just like Rosey and I support all of you!"

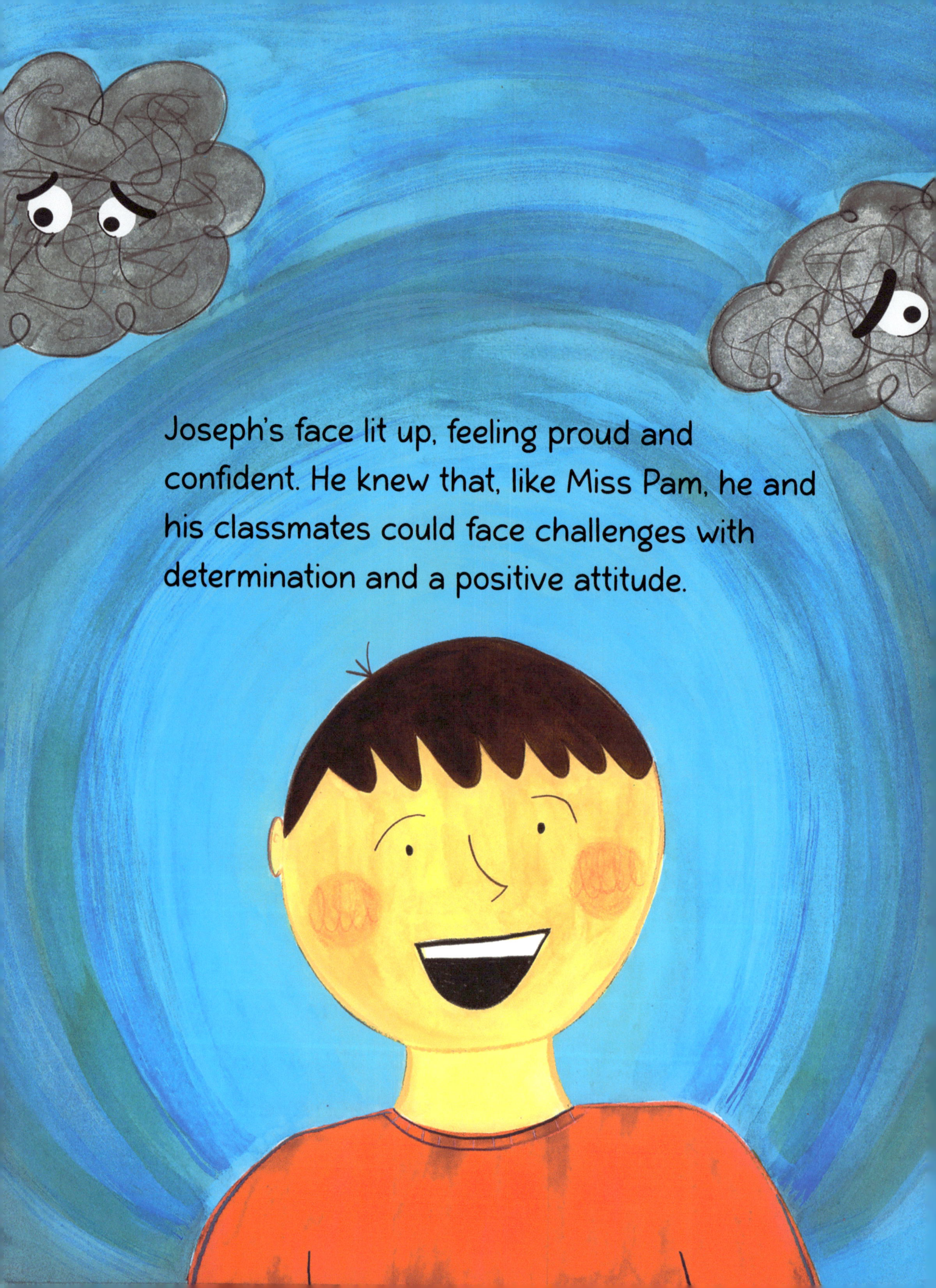

Joseph's face lit up, feeling proud and confident. He knew that, like Miss Pam, he and his classmates could face challenges with determination and a positive attitude.

"Now, is everyone ready for some warm-up music?" asked Miss Pam.

This time, everyone shouted,

Rosey barked because
she was ready, too!

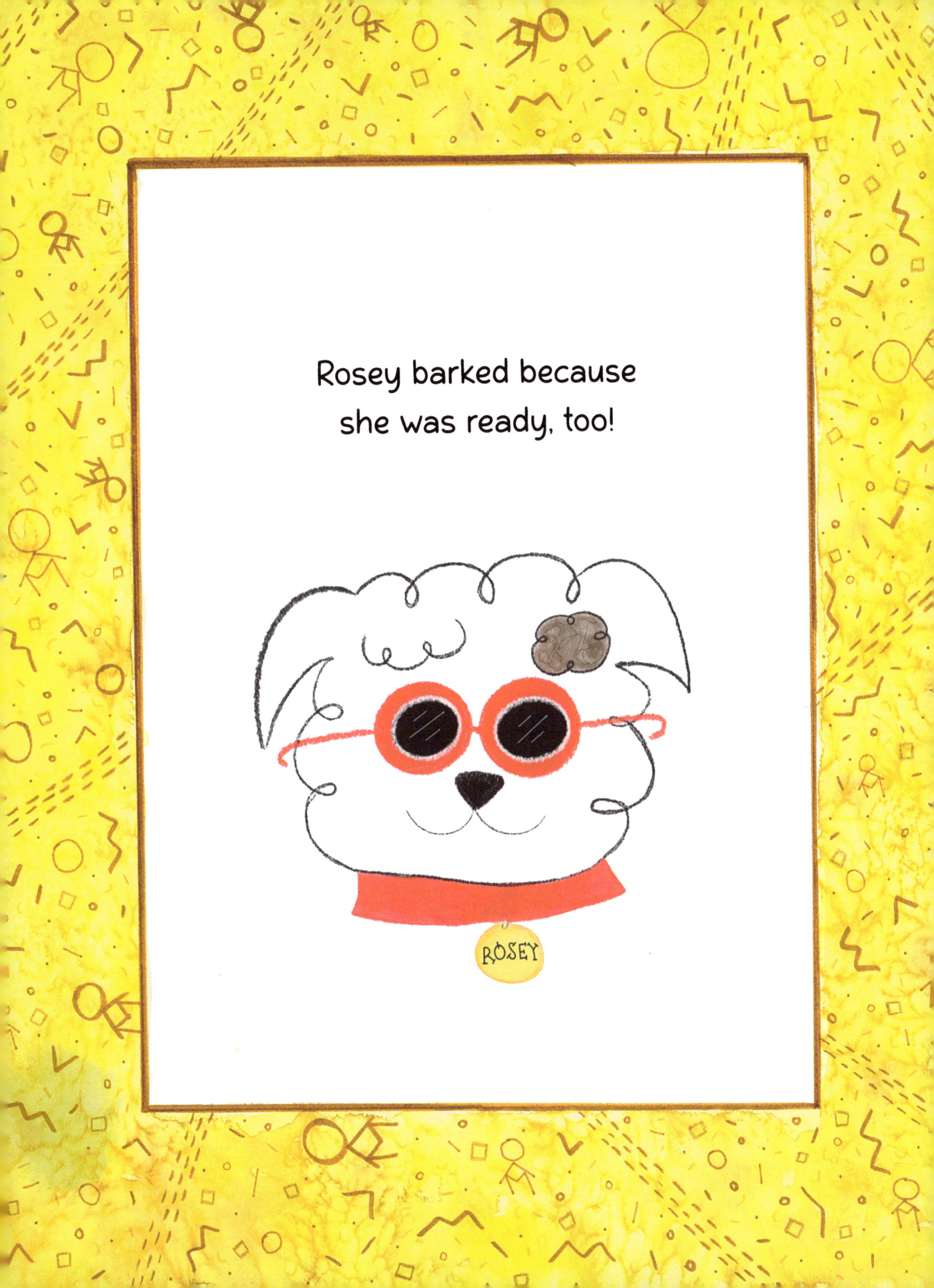

And so, the students at Bancroft Elementary always looked forward to PE class with Miss Pam and Rosey, knowing they would learn important life lessons about hope, positivity, and never giving up.

the
end

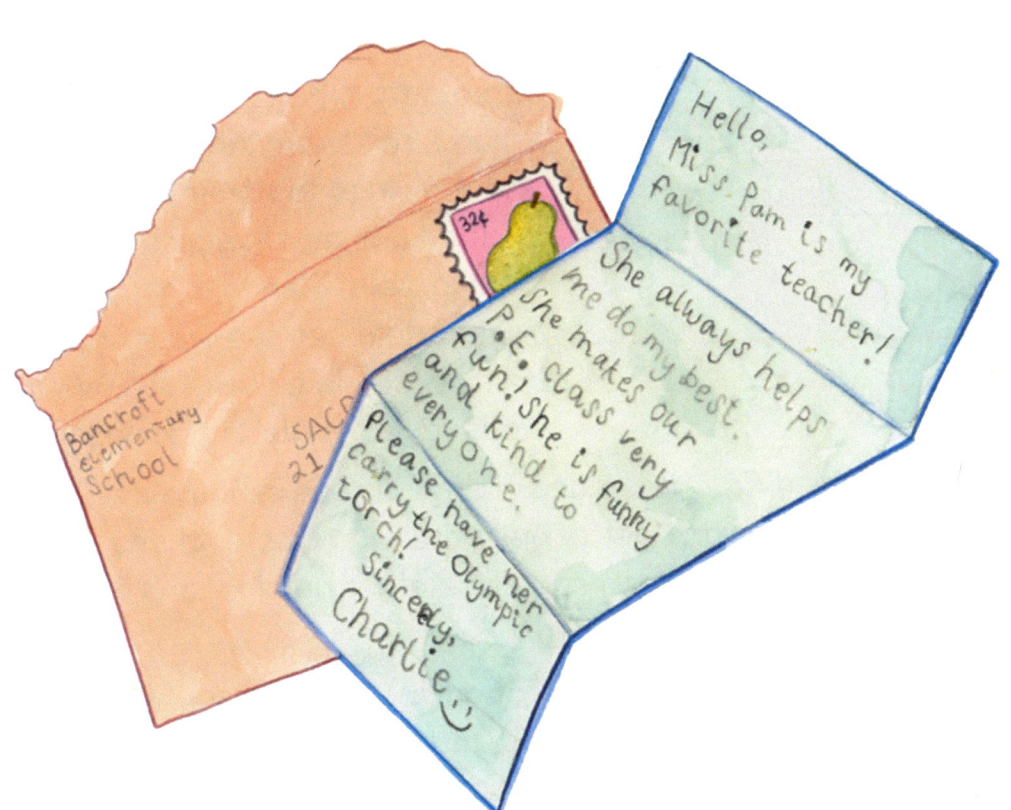

Pam Courtney: The Heart of the Olympic Spirit

Pam Courtney's life is a testament to the power of resilience, community, and an unyielding spirit. A Sacramento resident and physical education teacher at Bancroft Elementary School, she has become a beacon of inspiration, overcoming adversity and redefining what it means to embody the Olympic spirit.

Courtney once dreamed of competing as a cyclist in the 1988 Olympics, her ambitions fueled by a lifetime of athleticism. At just 10 years old, she tied for first place in track and field at the Junior Olympics. But in 1984 those dreams were shattered when a cross-country car trip turned tragic. Her boyfriend fell asleep at the wheel, overturning the car. Thrown from the vehicle, Courtney's back was broken, and she was left paralyzed.

In the face of such devastation, Courtney initially thought her Olympic aspirations were over. "I thought, *well, that's it. I'm never going to be a part of the Olympics*," she recalls. But her story was far from over.

In 1996, her students, colleagues, and parents from Bancroft Elementary School rallied around her, submitting heartfelt letters, essays, and drawings to nominate her as a torchbearer for the Summer Olympics. One parent, Jeanne Chasko, said, "Pam did not give up, although doctors told her she would never walk again. Her license plate reads 'IWL WALK' - she never stops for a minute to feel sorry for herself."

A young student named Caroline added, "Pam Courtney should get to carry the Olympic torch because she didn't get to be in the Olympics, and she's special. I love you, Pam." These words, coupled with countless other nominations, highlighted the depth of admiration Courtney had earned.

When she learned she had been chosen, Courtney was overwhelmed. "I feel so overwhelmed, excited, and thrilled," she said, tears in her eyes. "This has filled something that has been missing in my life, an inner void. All I can say is thank you."

Her journey did not stop there. In 2002, Courtney was selected again to carry the Olympic torch for the Winter Games in Salt Lake City. By then, she had spent years inspiring others through her teaching and as an advocate for accessibility. She was instrumental in persuading Arco Arena officials to raise seats, lower counters, install railings, and add Braille signs, creating a more inclusive environment for fans with disabilities.

At a school assembly announcing her selection, Courtney reflected on the moment. "It's a pretty awesome school I work for," she said with heartfelt gratitude. "To get a teaching job in a wheelchair was a huge thing, and to participate in the Olympics is really exciting."

For Courtney, her students remain at the heart of everything she does. "Seeing the kids, what they're capable of - it gives me inner strength," she said. "They are my life. I kind of feel like all the energy I've put out is now coming back to me."

Parents and colleagues echoed this sentiment. "Pam is an inspiration to all of us," said Cindi Anderson, a parent deeply involved in the nomination process. "She shows that no matter what life throws at you, you can make a difference and lift others in the process."

Today, Pam Courtney stands as a shining example of perseverance, gratitude, and the power of community. Her story is about overcoming physical limitations and channeling those challenges into a life of purpose and inspiration. With every step - or, in her case, every push of her wheelchair - she carries the flame of hope, lighting the way for those who look up to her.

"I always wanted to be in the Olympics," Courtney says. "This is my way of being a part of something extraordinary. It's not just about me - it's about all of us."

Pam's Final Graduation Speech, 2023.

Congratulations class of 2023!

I am so proud of you. I wish that I could be there with you in person, but please know that I am definitely there in spirit and so is Posey!

I loved attending all of your sporting events, piano recitals, and singing programs this year.

There was soccer, football, baseball, basketball, volleyball, swimming, and Running for Rhett. These runners ran a 5k in Old Sacramento in a relentless, soaking rainstorm.

I so enjoyed working with all the choreographers and dancers as their creative minds developed some amazing talent shows, "Bancroft Goes to Broadway." including *Hamilton*, and *Time Warp: A Musical Journey Through Time*. Whether you were working under the stage, backstage, or performing right on stage, you just constantly amazed and impressed me.

And kudos to you hard-working student council members, who worked student store, attended meetings, and worked Hall Monitor.

And how about that amazing toy and gift card drive that you worked both before and after school in December. I think about all of the kids and families that you made smile at Christmastime.

How fun it was watching you run in our annual Rudolph Run and the Beaver Dash, plus participate in all of the games throughout the years that we've played in PE - Including fencing with Master Nyteshade. And promise me you will never forget my good friend, Billy Bones.

You have been lucky to have some amazing teachers, staff, and an awesome principal over the years. And you gave a great sendoff to your longtime plant manager, Daryl.

I may have pushed you hard at times but it's because I believe in you! There is one thing you have total control over and that is your EFFORT! The kind of attitude you choose to have will open or close doors, and completely affect your life.

There are three kinds of people in this world, those who MAKE things happen, those who WATCH things happen, and those who WONDER what happened.

Words from the Broadway musical *Hamilton* says: DON'T THROW AWAY YOUR SHOT and IF YOU KEEP OUT OF TROUBLE YOU DOUBLE YOUR CHOICES. Take responsibility for your behavior, make smart choices, and be a person who makes things happen.

Don't forget to run and dance and laugh and pay it forward. Be kind to one another and help make the world a better place. And to those of you familiar with *America's Got Talent* ... Class of 2023, you are my Golden Buzzer!

I'm going to miss you!

The Pam Courtney Foundation Memorial Fund
Continuing the Light of "Miss Pam"

Pam Courtney was more than a teacher. She was a force of joy, resilience, and unconditional love. As a P.E. teacher in a wheelchair, a two-time Olympic torch bearer, and a tireless champion for her students and community, Miss Pam inspired generations of children to move, create, lead, and love without limits.

The Pam Courtney Foundation was created to carry her light forward.

With every *Miss Pam's Here!* book purchased, you are supporting this mission. Proceeds go to the foundation's programs, which include:

- Offsetting sports and arts participation fees for families in the College Glen community

- Supporting Bancroft Elementary talent shows and school events that Pam once led with her whole heart

- Funding future scholarships for Bancroft students pursuing education, sports, or the arts

- Nurturing community spirit through events like the Pam Courtney Jamboree and student-run initiatives, which Pam held dear.

We invite you to keep Miss Pam's light shining by donating. Every dollar makes a difference. To learn more or contribute, visit:

www.facebook.com/PamCourtneyFoundation

www.pamcourtneyfoundation.org

"It's not about how much you give, but how much love you put into giving."

- Pam Courtney

About The Author - Dan Freschi

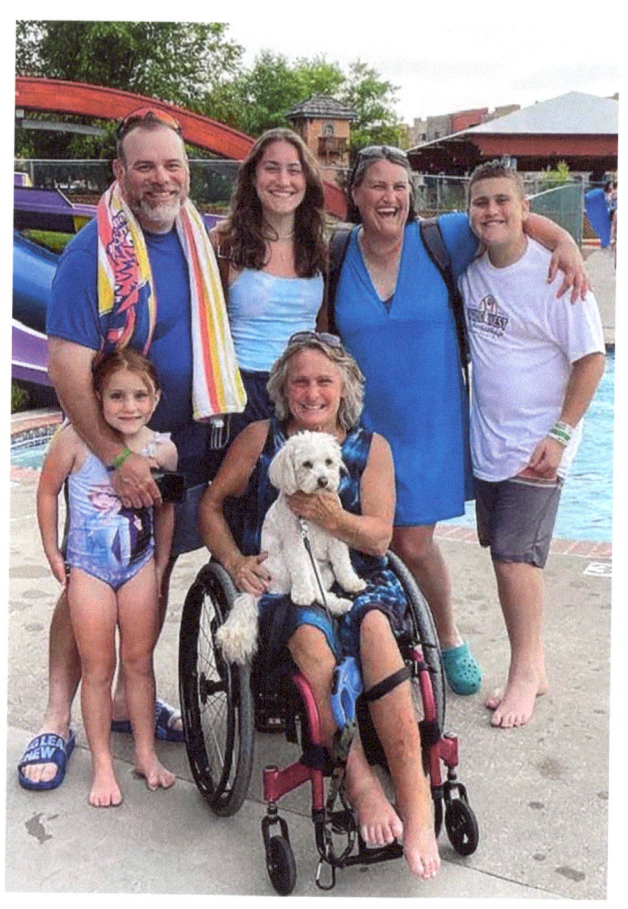

Dan Freschi is the proud nephew of the late Pam Courtney, known to many as Miss Pam, Aunt Pam, or simply the heart of Hubert H. Bancroft Elementary. Her influence runs deep in Dan's life - not only shaping his personal values but also guiding his career, parenting, and sense of purpose.

Dan created the *Miss Pam's Here!* series to bring his Aunt Pam's timeless lessons to life. Her courage, humor, joy, and fierce love for others left an imprint on everyone she met, but no one more than Dan. After high school, Pam welcomed him into her Sacramento home and encouraged him to attend Sacramento State. She cheered him through every milestone that followed, including his service in the U.S. Army, his teaching career, and his life as a husband and father.

Today, Dan lives in Wisconsin with his wife, Kecia, and their three children, Claire, Chase, and Chloe, who all knew Pam not just as a family member, but also as their biggest cheerleader. Weekly calls with "Aunt Pam" were filled with stories, laughter, love, and life advice. Her legacy lives on in their home, through the way they show up for others, face challenges with grit, and live life with heart.

Dan is an Army veteran, a leadership educator, and an adjunct professor at Carroll University. He also leads a nonprofit youth baseball program, teaching character, resilience, and leadership to student-athletes and professionals alike. Through the Pam Courtney Foundation, Dan and his family continue the work Pam started, supporting children in sports, the arts, and education in her beloved College Glen community and beyond.

Pam's voice continues to guide him. This series is Dan's way of making sure it never stops inspiring the world.

To learn more or get involved, visit:

www.pamcourtneyfoundation.org

www.whereleadershipbegins.com

www.misspamshere.com

About The Illustrator - Angela Ayala

Angela is an arts and crafts enthusiast who can often be found painting, collaging, or sewing. She is a graduate of CSU Sacramento where she earned a bachelor's degree in humanities. Angela has worked with students of all ages, the California State government, and at Sacramento's finest movie palaces. She resides in the Camellia City with her husband and cats.

Miss Pam was and will forever be Angela's favorite teacher.

For more about Angela, visit her website:

www.hotpresspaperdoll.com/